Creature Comparisons

Snakes

Tracey Crawford

Heinemann Library
Chicago, Illinois

Photo research by Tracy Cummins, Tracey Engel, and Ruth Blair
Designed by Jo Hinton-Malivoire
Printed and bound in China by South China Printing Company
10 09 08
10 9 8 7 6 5 4 3

Library of Congress Cataloging-in-Publication Data
Crawford, Tracey.
   Snakes / Tracey Crawford.— 1st ed.
      p. cm. — (Creature comparisons)
   Includes bibliographical references and index.
   ISBN-13: 978-1-4034-8452-9 (hc) ISBN-10: 1-4034-8452-X (hc)
   ISBN-13: 978-1-4034-8459-8 (pb) ISBN-10: 1-4034-8459-7 (pb)
   1. Snakes—Juvenile literature. I. Title. II. Series.
   QL666.O6C824 2007
   597.96—dc22
                              2006007668

Acknowledgments
The author and publisher are grateful to the following for permission to reproduce copyright material: Corbis pp. **4** (monkey, Frank Lukasseck/zefa; bird, Arthur Morris), **9** (Michael & Patricia Fogden), **12** (Theo Allofs), **13**, **15** (Michael & Patricia Fogden), **22** (Horned Adder, Gallo Images; rattlesnake, Jeff Vanuga); Getty Images pp. **4** (fish), **7** (Jim Merli), **10** (The Image Bank/Gallo Images-Anthony Bannister), **23** (king snake, Jim Merli; hatchling, The Image Bank/Gallo Images-Anthony Bannister); Minden Pictures pp. **11** (Michael & Patricia Fogden); Carlton Ward pp. **4** (frog), **5**, **6**, **14**, **16**, **17**, **18**, **19**, **20**, **21**, **23** (viper headshot).

Cover photograph of an emerald tree boa reproduced with permission of Corbis/Joe MacDonald and an Indian cobra reproduced with permission of Ardea/M. Watson. Back cover photograph of a banded sea snake reproduced with permission of Corbis.

Every effort has been made to contact copyright holders of any material reproduced in this book.
Any omissions will be rectified in subsequent printings if notice is given to the publisher.

Contents

There are many types of animals.

Snakes are one type of animal.

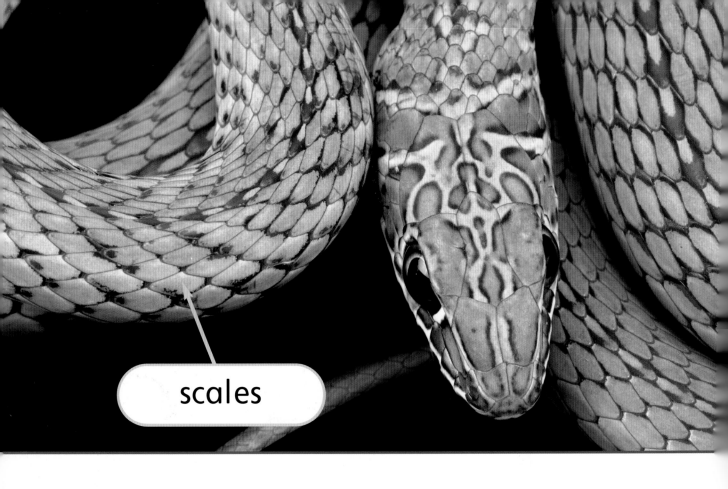

scales

All snakes have scales.

All snakes shed their skin.

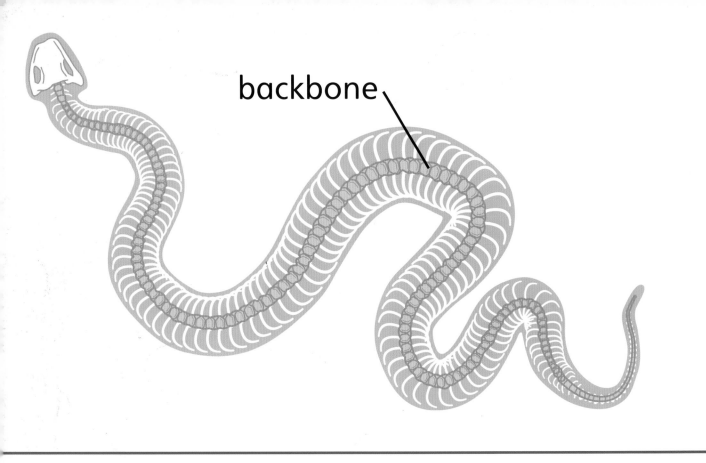

backbone

All snakes have a backbone.

All snakes hunt for food.

Most snakes hatch from an egg.

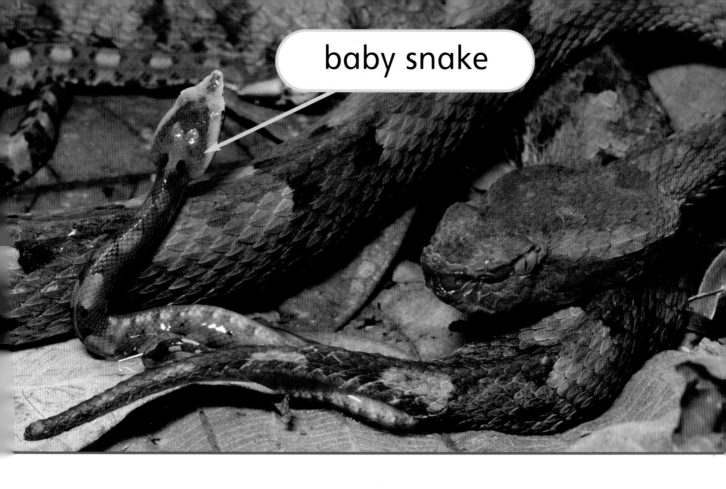

baby snake

But this snake does not.

Most snakes live on land.

But this snake does not.

Some snakes are big.

Some snakes are small.

Some snakes are smooth.

Some snakes are rough.

Some snakes are one color.

Some snakes are many colors.

Every snake is different.

Every snake is special.

Snake Facts

Snakes cannot hear. Snakes can feel movement.

This snake is a horned viper. It hides itself in the sand.

Picture Glossary

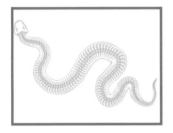

backbone the part of the skeleton that goes from the head to the tail

hatch to be born from an egg

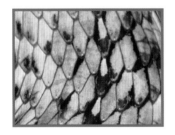

scale a small, flat plate on the outside of an animal. Scales cover skin.

shed to take off

Index

Note to Parents and Teachers

In *Snakes*, children are introduced to the diversity found within this animal group, as well as the characteristics that all snakes share. The text has been carefully chosen with the advice of a literacy expert to enable beginning readers success while reading independently or with moderate support. Scientists were consulted to provide both interesting and accurate content.

By showing the importance of diversity within wildlife, *Snakes* invites children to welcome diversity in their own lives. The book ends by stating that every snake is a unique, special creature. Use this as a discussion point for how each person is also unique and special. You can support children's nonfiction literacy skills by helping them to use the table of contents, picture glossary, and index.